IS ALL SCRIPTURE
INSPIRED?

IS ALL SCRIPTURE
INSPIRED?

J. C. Ryle

THE BANNER OF TRUTH TRUST

THE BANNER OF TRUTH TRUST
3 Murrayfield Road, Edinburgh EH12 6EL
P.O. Box 621, Carlisle, Pennsylvania 17013, USA

*

First published in *Old Paths* [1878], reprinted 1999
First edition in this form 2003

*

ISBN 0 85151 848 6

*

Typeset in 12/18 pt Galliard at the
Banner of Truth Trust, Edinburgh
Printed and bound in Great Britain by
Creative Print & Design (Wales),
Ebbw Vale

Contents

[v]

Publisher's Preface

When J. C. Ryle published *Old Paths, being Plain Statements on Some of the Weightier Matters of Christianity*, in 1878, he deliberately placed a paper on *Inspiration* at the beginning of the volume. To him the inspiration of the Scriptures was 'the very keel and foundation of Christianity', without which Christians had no warrant for doctrine or practice, 'no solid ground for present peace or hope, and no right to claim the attention of mankind'.

The publishers believe that Ryle's brief treatment of the subject is of permanent value and well worth making available separately in this more accessible form.

Ryle added a series of quotations on inspiration by four representative theologians, and we have retained these as Appendix 1. As a further Appendix, we have included an address by Ryle on 'Not Corrupting the Word', previously published in *Warnings to the Churches*.

October 2003

1

Introduction

'All scripture is given by inspiration of God'
(*2 Tim.* 3:16).

How was the Bible written? 'Whence is it? From
heaven, or of men?' Had the writers of the
Bible any special or peculiar help in doing their work? Is
there anything in the Bible which makes it unlike
all other books, and therefore demands our respectful
attention? These are questions of vast importance. They
are questions to which I wish to offer an answer in this
paper. To speak plainly, the subject I propose to examine is
that deep one, *the inspiration of Scripture*. I believe the
Bible to have been written by inspiration of God, and I
want others to be of the same belief.

The subject is *always important*. I place it purposely in the very forefront of the papers which compose this volume.[1] I ask a hearing for the doctrines which I am about to handle, because they are drawn from a book which is the 'Word of God'. Inspiration, in short, is the very keel and foundation of Christianity. If Christians have no divine book to turn to as the warrant of their doctrine and practice, they have no solid ground for present peace or hope, and no right to claim the attention of mankind. They are building on a quicksand, and their faith is vain. We ought to be able to say boldly, 'We are what we are, and we do what we do, because we have here a book which we believe to be the Word of God.'

The subject is one of *peculiar importance* in the present day. Infidelity and scepticism abound everywhere. In one form or another they are to be found in every rank and class of society. Thousands of Englishmen are not ashamed to say that they regard the Bible as an old obsolete Jewish book, which has no special claim on our faith and obedience, and that it contains many inaccuracies and defects. Myriads who will not go so far as this are wavering and shaken in their belief, and show plainly by their lives that they are not quite sure the Bible is true. In a day like this the true Christian should be able to set his foot down firmly, and to render a reason of his confidence in God's Word.

[1] The reference is to *Old Paths* (1878; reprinted Edinburgh: Banner of Truth, 1999), where this paper originally appeared.

He should be able by sound arguments to meet and silence the gainsayer, if he cannot convince him. He should be able to (show good cause) why he thinks the Bible is 'from heaven, and not of men'.

The subject without doubt is a *very difficult one*. It cannot be followed up without entering on ground which is dark and mysterious to mortal man. It involves the discussion of things which are miraculous, and supernatural, and above reason, and cannot be fully explained. But difficulties must not turn us away from any subject in religion. There is not a science in the world about which questions may not be asked which no one can answer. It is poor philosophy to say we will believe nothing unless we can understand everything! We must not give up the subject of inspiration in despair because it contains things 'hard to be understood'. There still remains a vast amount of ground which is plain to every common understanding. I invite my readers to occupy this ground with me today, and to hear what I have to say on the divine authority of God's Word.

In considering the subject before us, there are two things which I propose to do:

1. In the first place, I shall try to show the general truth, that *the Bible is given by inspiration of God.*

2. In the second place, I shall try to show *the extent to which the Bible is inspired.*

I trust that all who read this paper will take up the subject in a serious and reverent spirit. This question of inspiration is no light one. It involves tremendously grave consequences. If the Bible is not the Word of God and inspired, the whole of Christendom for 1800 years has been under an immense delusion; half the human race has been cheated and deceived, and churches are monuments of folly. If the Bible is the Word of God and inspired, all who refuse to believe it are in fearful danger; they are living on the brink of eternal misery. No man, in his sober senses, can fail to see that the whole subject demands most serious attention.

2

The Bible Is Inspired

In the first place, I propose to show the general truth that the Bible is given by inspiration of God.

In saying this I mean to assert that the Bible is utterly unlike all other books that were ever written because its writers were specially inspired, or enabled by God, for the work which they did. I say that the Book comes to us with a claim which no other book possesses. It is stamped with divine authority. In this respect it stands entirely alone. Sermons, and tracts, and theological writings of all kinds, may be sound and edifying but they are only the handiwork of uninspired man. The Bible alone is the Book of God.

Now I shall not waste time in proving that the Scriptures are genuine and authentic, that they were really written by the very men who profess to have written them, and that they contain the very things which they wrote. I shall not touch what are commonly called external evidences. I shall bring forward the book itself, and put it in the witness box. I shall try to show that nothing can possibly account for the Bible being what it is, and doing what it has done, except the theory that it is the Word of God.

I lay it down broadly, as a position which cannot be turned, that the Bible itself, fairly examined, is the best witness of its own inspiration. I shall content myself with stating some plain facts about the Bible which can neither be denied nor explained away. And the ground I shall take up is this, that these facts ought to satisfy every reasonable inquirer that the Bible is of God, and not of man. They are simple facts which require no knowledge of Hebrew or Greek or Latin in order to be understood; yet they are facts which prove to my own mind conclusively that the Bible is superhuman, or not of man.

1. The Richness of the Bible's Contents

It is a fact that there is an *extraordinary fullness and richness in the contents of the Bible*. It throws more light on a vast number of most important subjects than all the other books in the world put together. It boldly handles matters which are beyond the reach of man, when left to himself. It treats of things which are mysterious and invisible – the soul, the world to come, and eternity – depths which man has no line to fathom. All who have tried to write of these things, without Bible light, have done little but show their own ignorance. They grope like the blind; they speculate; they guess; they generally make the darkness more visible, and land us in a region of uncertainty and doubt. How dim were the views of Socrates, Plato, Cicero, and Seneca! A well-taught Sunday scholar, in this day, knows more spiritual truth than all these sages put together.

The Bible alone gives a reasonable account of *the begin-ning and end of the globe* on which we live. It starts from the birthday of sun, moon, stars, and earth in their present order, and shows us creation in its cradle. It foretells the dissolution of all things, when the earth and all its works shall be burned up, and shows us creation in its grave. It tells us the story of the world's youth; and it tells us the story of its old age. It gives us a picture of its first days; and it gives us a picture of its last. How vast and important is this knowledge! Can this be the handiwork of uninspired man? Let us try to answer that question.

The Bible alone gives a *true and faithful account of man.* It does not flatter him as novels and romances do; it does not conceal his faults and exaggerate his goodness; it paints him just as he is. It describes him as a fallen creature, of his own nature inclined to evil, a creature needing not only a pardon but a new heart to make him fit for heaven. It shows him to be a corrupt being under every circumstance, when left to himself – corrupt after the loss of paradise, corrupt after the flood, corrupt when fenced in by divine laws and commandments, corrupt when the Son of God came down and visited him in the flesh, corrupt in the face of warnings, promises, miracles, judgments, mercies. In one word it shows man to be by nature always a sinner. How important is this knowledge! Can this be the work of uninspired minds? Let us try to answer that question.

The Bible alone gives us *true views of God*. By nature man knows nothing clearly or fully about Him. All his conceptions of Him are low, grovelling, and debased. What could be more degraded than the gods of the Canaanites and Egyptians, of Babylon, of Greece, and of Rome? What can be more vile than the gods of the Hindus and other heathen in our own time? By the Bible we know that *God hates sin*. The destruction of the old world by the flood; the burning of Sodom and Gomorrah; the drowning of Pharaoh and the Egyptians in the Red Sea; the cutting off the nations of Canaan; the overthrow of Jerusalem and the Temple; the scattering of the Jews – all these are unmistakable witnesses. By the Bible we know that *God loves sinners*. His gracious promise in the day of Adam's fall; His longsuffering in the time of Noah; His deliverance of Israel out of the land of Egypt; His gift of the law at Mount Sinai; His bringing the tribes into the promised land; His forbearance in the days of the Judges and Kings; His repeated warnings by the mouth of His prophets; His restoration of Israel after the Babylonian captivity; His sending His Son into the world, in due time, to be crucified; His commanding the gospel to be preached to the Gentiles; all these are speaking facts.

By the Bible we learn that *God knows all things.* We see Him foretelling things hundreds and thousands of years before they take place, and as He foretells, so it comes to pass. He foretold that the family of Ham should be a servant of servants, that Tyre should become a rock for drying nets, that Nineveh should become a desolation, that Babylon should be made a desert, that Egypt should be the basest of kingdoms, that Edom should be forsaken and uninhabited, and that the Jews should not be reckoned among the nations. All these things were utterly unlikely and improbable. Yet all have been fulfilled. Once more I say, how vast and important is all this knowledge! Can this Book be the work of uninspired man? Let us try to answer that question.

The Bible alone teaches us that *God has made a full, perfect, and complete provision for the salvation of fallen man.* It tells of an atonement made for the sin of the world, by the sacrifice and death of God's own Son upon the cross. It tells us that by His death for sinners, as their Substitute, He obtained eternal redemption for all that believe on Him.

The claims of God's broken law have now been satisfied. Christ has suffered for sin, the just for the unjust. God can now be just, and yet the justifier of the ungodly. It tells us that there is now a complete remedy for the guilt of sin, even the precious blood of Christ; and peace, and rest of conscience for all who believe on Christ. 'Whosoever believeth on Him shall not perish, but have everlasting life.' It tells us that there is a complete remedy for the power of sin, even the almighty grace of the Spirit of Christ. It shows us the Holy Ghost quickening believers, and making them new creatures. It promises a new heart and a new nature to all who will hear Christ's voice, and follow Him. Once more I say, how important is this knowledge! What should we know of all this comfortable truth without the Bible? Can this Book be the composition of uninspired men? Let us try to answer that question.

The Bible alone *explains the state of things that we see in the world around us.* There are many things on earth which a natural man cannot explain. The amazing inequality of conditions, the poverty and distress, the oppression and persecution, the shakings and tumults, the failures of states-men and legislators, the constant existence of uncured evils and abuses, all these things are often puzzling to him. He sees, but does not understand. But the Bible makes it all clear.

The Bible can tell him that the whole world lieth in wickedness, that the prince of the world, the devil, is everywhere, and that it is vain to look for perfection in the present order of things. The Bible will tell him that neither laws nor education can ever change men's hearts, and that just as no man will ever make a machine work well unless he allows for friction, so also no man will do much good in the world unless he always remembers that human nature is fallen, and that the world he works in is full of sin.

The Bible will tell him that there is 'a good time' certainly coming, and coming perhaps sooner than people expect it, a time of perfect knowledge, perfect justice, perfect happiness, and perfect peace.

But the Bible will tell him this time shall not be brought in by any power but that of Christ coming to earth again. And for that second coming of Christ, the Bible will tell him to prepare. Once more, I say, how important is all this knowledge! All these are things which men could find nowhere except in the Scriptures. We have probably not the least idea how little we should know about these things if we had not the Bible.

We hardly know the value of the air we breathe, and the sun which shines on us, because we have never known what it is to be without them. We do not value the truths on which I have been just now dwelling because we do not realize the darkness of men to whom these truths have not been revealed. Surely no tongue can fully tell the value of the treasures this one volume contains. Set down that fact in your mind, and do not forget it. The extraordinary contents of the Bible are a great fact which can only be explained by admitting its inspiration. Mark well what I say. It is a simple broad fact that, in the matter of its contents, the Bible stands entirely alone, and no other book is fit to be named in the same day with it, He that dares to say the Bible is not inspired, let him give a reasonable account of this fact, if he can.

2. The Unity and Harmony of the Bible's Contents

It is another fact that there is an extraordinary unity and harmony in the contents of the Bible which is entirely above man. We all know how difficult it is to get a story told by any three persons, not living together, in which there are not some contradictions and discrepancies. If the story is a long one, and involves a large quantity of particulars, unity seems almost impossible among the common run of men. But it is not so with the Bible.

Here is a long book written by not less than thirty different persons. The writers were men of every rank and class in society. One was a lawgiver. One was a warlike king. One was a peaceful king. One was a herdsman. One had been brought up as a publican, another as a physician, another as a learned Pharisee, two as fishermen, several as priests. They lived at different intervals over a space of 1500 years; and the greater part of them never saw each other face to face. And yet there is a perfect harmony among all these writers! They all write as if they were under one dictation. The style and hand-writing may vary, but the mind that runs through their work is always one and the same. They all tell the same story. They all give one account of man, one account of God, one account of the way of salvation, one account of the human heart. You see truth unfolding under their hands, as you get through the volume of their writings, but you never detect any real contradiction or contrariety of view.

Let us set down this fact in our minds, and ponder it well. Tell us not that this unity might be the result of chance. No one can ever believe that but a very credulous person. There is only one satisfactory account to be given of the fact before us. The Bible is not of man, but of God.

3. The Majesty of the Bible's Style

It is another fact that there is an extraordinary wisdom, sublimity and majesty in the style of the Bible which is above man. Strange and unlikely as it was, the writers of Scripture have produced a book which even at this day is utterly unrivalled. With all our boasted attainments in science and art and learning, we can produce nothing that can be compared with the Bible. Even at this very hour, in 1877, the book stands entirely alone.

There is a strain and a style and a tone of thought about it, which separate it from all other writings. There are no weak points, motes, flaws and blemishes. There is no mixture of infirmity and feebleness, such as you will find in the works of even the best Christians. 'Holy, holy, holy', seems written on every page. To talk of comparing the Bible with other 'sacred books' so-called, such as the Koran, the Shastras, or the book of Mormon, is positively absurd. You might as well compare the sun with a rushlight, or Skiddaw with a mole hill, or St Paul's with an Irish hovel, or the Portland vase with a garden pot, or the Koh-i-noor diamond with a bit of glass.[1]

God seems to have allowed the existence of these pretended revelations, in order to prove the immeasurable superiority of His own Word.[2] To talk of the inspiration of the Bible as only differing *in degree* from that of such writings as the works of Homer, Plato, Shakespeare, Dante and Milton is simply a piece of blasphemous folly. Every

[1] Thomas Carlyle's estimate of the Koran is given, in his *Hero-worship*, in the following words: 'It is a wearisome, confused jumble, crude, recondite, abounding in endless iterations, long-windedness, entanglement, insupportable stupidity. In short nothing but a sense of duty could carry any European through the Koran, with its unreadable masses of lumber.'

[2] John Owen says, 'There is no other writing extant in the world [beside the Bible] that ever pretended unto a divine original . . . but they are, not only from their matter, but from the manner of their writing, and the plain footsteps of human artifice and weakness therein, sufficient for their own conviction, and do openly discover their own vain pretensions.' 'The Reason of Faith' in *Works*, vol 4, p. 34 (London: Banner of Truth, 1967).

honest and unprejudiced reader must see that there is a gulf between the Bible and any other book which no man can fathom.

You feel, on turning from the Scriptures to other works, that you have got into a new atmosphere. You feel like one who has exchanged gold for base metal, and heaven for earth. And how can this mighty difference be accounted for? The men who wrote the Bible had no special advantages. They lived in a remote corner of the civilized earth. They had, most of them, little leisure, few books, and no learning, such as learning is reckoned in this world. Yet the book they compose is one which is unrivalled! There is but one way of accounting for this fact: *They wrote under the direct inspiration of God.*

4. The Accuracy of the Bible's Statements

It is another fact that there is an extraordinary accuracy in the facts and statements of the Bible which is above man. Here is a book which has been finished and before the world for nearly 1800 years. These 1800 years have been the busiest and most changeful period the world has ever seen. During this period the greatest discoveries have been made in science, the greatest alterations in the ways and customs of society, the greatest improvements in the habits and usages of life. Hundreds of things might be named which satisfied and pleased our forefathers, which we have laid aside long ago as obsolete, useless, and old-fashioned. The laws, the books, the houses, the furniture, the clothes, the arms, the machinery, the carriages of each succeeding century, have been a continual improvement on those of the century that went before.

There is hardly a thing in which faults and weak points have not been discovered. There is scarcely an institution which has not gone through a process of sifting, purifying, refining, simplifying, reforming, amending, and changing. But all this time men have never discovered a weak point or a defect in the Bible. Infidels have assailed it in vain. There it stands, perfect, and fresh, and complete, as it did eighteen centuries ago.

The march of intellect never overtakes it. The wisdom of wise men never gets beyond it. The science of philosophers never proves it wrong. The discoveries of travellers never convict it of mistakes. Are the distant islands of the Pacific laid open? Nothing is found that in the slightest degree contradicts the Bible account of man's heart. Are the ruins of Nineveh and Egypt ransacked and explored? Nothing is found that overturns one jot or tittle of the Bible's historical statements. How shall we account for this fact?

Who could have thought it possible that so large a book, handling such a vast variety of subjects, should at the end of 1800 years, be found so free from erroneous statements? There is only one account to be given of the fact. The Bible was *written by inspiration of God*.

5. The Bible's Suitability to the Needs of Mankind

It is another fact that there is in the Bible an extraordinary suitableness to the spiritual wants of all mankind. It exactly meets the heart of man in every rank or class, in every country and climate, in every age and period of life. It is the only book in existence which is never out of place and out of date.

Other books after a time become obsolete and old-fashioned: the Bible never does. Other books suit one country or people, and not another: the Bible suits all. It is the book of the poor and unlearned no less than of the rich and the philosopher. It feeds the mind of the labourer in his cottage, and it satisfies the gigantic intellects of Newton, Chalmers, Brewster, and Faraday. Lord Macaulay, and John Bright, and the writers of brilliant articles in *The Times*, are all under obligations to the same volume. It is equally valued by the converted New Zealander in the southern hemisphere, and the Red River Indian in the cold north of America, and the Hindu under the tropical sun.

It is the only book, moreover, which seems always fresh and evergreen and new. For eighteen centuries it has been studied and prayed over by millions of private Christians, and expounded and explained and preached to us by thousands of ministers. Fathers, and Schoolmen, and Reformers, and Puritans, and modern divines, have incessantly dug down into the mine of Scripture, and yet have never exhausted it. It is a well never dry, and a field which is never barren. It meets the hearts and minds and consciences of Christians in the nineteenth century as fully as it did those of Greeks and Romans when it was first completed. It suits the 'Dairyman's daughter' as well as Persis, or Tryphena, or Tryphosa, and the English Peer as well as the converted African in Sierra Leone. It is still the first book which fits the child's mind when he begins to learn religion, and the last to which the old man clings as he leaves the world.[1] In short, it suits all ages, ranks, climates, minds, conditions. It is the one book which suits the world.

[1] 'I have always been strongly in favour of secular education in the sense of education without theology. But I must confess I have been no less seriously perplexed to know by what practical measures the religious feeling, which is the essential basis of conduct could be kept up in the present chaotic state of opinion on these matters without the use of the Bible.

'Consider the great historical fact that for three centuries this Book has been woven into the life of all that is best and noblest in English history, that it has become the national epic of Britain, and is as familiar to noble and simple from John o' Groat's Home to the Land's End, as Dante and Tasso once were to the Italians; that it is written in the best and purest English, and abounds in exquisite beauties of mere literary form; and finally, that it forbids the veriest hind who never left his village to be ignorant of other countries and other civilizations, and of a great past, stretching back to the furthest limits of the oldest nations in the world. By the study of what other book could children be so much humanized and made to feel that each figure in that vast

Now how shall we account for this singular fact? What satisfactory explanation can we give? There is only one account and explanation. The Bible was written by divine inspiration. It is the book of the world because He inspired it who formed the world, who made all nations of one blood, and knows man's common nature. It is the book for every heart because He dictated it who alone knows all hearts, and what all hearts require. It is the book of God.

6. The Effects of a Knowledge of the Bible

Last, but not least, it is a great fact that the Bible has had a most extraordinary effect on the condition of those nations in which it has been known, taught, and read.

I invite any honest-minded reader to look at a map of the world, and see what a story that map tells. Which are the countries on the face of the globe at this moment where there is the greatest amount of idolatry, or cruelty, or tyranny, or impurity, or misgovernment, or disregard of life and liberty and truth? Precisely those countries where

---

historical procession fills, like themselves, but a momentary space in the interval between two eternities, and earns the blessing or the curses of all time, according to its effort to do good and hate evil even as they also are earning their payment for their work?' *Professor Huxley on School Boards* (*Huxley's Critiques and Essays*, p. 51).

the Bible is not known. Which are the Christian countries, so-called, where the greatest quantity of ignorance, superstition, and corruption, is to be found at this very moment? The countries in which the Bible is a forbidden or neglected book, such countries as Spain and the South American States. Which are the countries where liberty, and public and private morality have attained the highest pitch? The countries where the Bible is free to all, like England, Scotland, Germany, and the United States. Yes! when you know how a nation deals with the Bible, you may generally know what a nation is.

But this is not all. Let us look nearer home. Which are the cities on earth where the fewest soldiers and police are required to keep order? London, Manchester, Liverpool, New York, Philadelphia, cities where Bibles abound. Which are the countries in Europe where there are the fewest murders and illegitimate births? The Protestant countries, where the Bible is freely read.

Which are the Churches and religious bodies on earth which are producing the greatest results by spreading light and dispelling darkness? Those which make much of the Bible, and teach and preach it as God's Word. The Romanist, the Neologian, the Socinian, the deist, the sceptic, or the friends of mere secular teaching, have never yet shown us one Sierra Leone, one New Zealand, one Tinnevelly, as the fruit of their principles. We only can do that who honour the Bible and reverence it as God's Word.

Let this fact also be remembered. He that denies the divine inspiration of the Bible, let him explain this fact if he can.[1]

I place these six facts about the Bible before my readers, and I ask them to consider them well. Take them all six together, treat them fairly, and look at them honestly. Upon any other principle than that of divine inspiration, those six facts appear to me inexplicable and unaccountable. Here is a book written by a succession of Jews, in a little corner of the world, which positively stands alone. Not only were its writers isolated and cut off in a peculiar manner from other nations, but they belonged to a people who have never produced any other book of note except the Bible! There is not the slightest proof that, unassisted and left to themselves, they were capable of writing anything remarkable, like the Greeks and Romans. Yet these men have given the world a volume which for depth, unity, sublimity, accuracy, suitableness to the wants of man, and power of influencing its readers, is perfectly unrivalled. How can this

[1] 'The Bible is the fountain of all true patriotism and loyalty in states. It is the source of all true wisdom, sound policy, and equity in Senates, Council-chambers, and Courts of Justice. It is the spring of all true discipline and obedience, and of all valour and chivalry, in armies and fleets, in the battlefield and on the wide sea. It is the origin of all probity and integrity in commerce and in trade, in marts and in shops, in banks and exchanges, in the public resorts of men and the secret silence of the heart. It is the pure, unsullied fountain of all love and peace, happiness, quietness and joy, in families and households. Wherever it is duly obeyed it makes the desert of the world to rejoice and blossom as the rose' (Wordsworth on *Inspiration*, p. 113).

be explained? How can it be accounted for? To my mind there is only one answer. The writers of the Bible were divinely helped and qualified for the work which they did. The book which they have given to us was written by inspiration of God.[1]

For my own part, I believe that in dealing with sceptics, and unbelievers, and enemies of the Bible, Christians are too apt to stand only on the defensive. They are too often content with answering this or that little objection, or discussing this or that little difficulty, which is picked out of Scripture and thrown in their teeth. I believe we ought to act on the aggressive far more than we do, and to press home on the adversaries of inspiration the enormous difficulties of their own position.

We have a right to ask them how they can possibly explain the origin and nature of the Bible, if they will not allow that it is of divine authority. We have a right to say, 'Here is a book which not only courts inquiry but demands investigation. We challenge you to tell us how that Book was written.' How can they account for this Book standing so entirely alone, and for nothing having ever been written equal to it, like it, near it, or fit to be compared with it for a minute? I defy them to give, any rational reply

'The little ark of Jewish literature still floats above the surges of time, while mere fragments of the wrecked archives of the huge oriental empires, as well as of the lesser kingdoms that surrounded Judaea are now and then cast on our distant shores' (Rogers on *The Superhuman Origin of the Bible*, p. 311).

on their own principles. On our principles we can. To tell us that man's unassisted mind could have written the Bible is simply ridiculous. It is worse than ridiculous: it is the height of credulity.

In short, the difficulties of unbelief are far greater than the difficulties of faith. No doubt there are things 'hard to be understood' if we accept the Scriptures as God's Word. But, after all, they are nothing compared to the hard things which rise up in our way, and demand solution if we once deny inspiration. There is no alternative. Men must either believe things which are grossly improbable, or else they must accept the great general truth that the Bible is the inspired Word of God.

3

Every Word of the Bible Is Inspired

The second thing which I propose to consider is the extent to which the Bible is inspired. Assuming, as a general truth, that the Bible is given by divine inspiration, I wish to examine how far and to what degree its writers received divine help. In short, what is it exactly that we mean when we talk of the Scriptures as ' the Word of God'?

Inspiration Is Miraculous

This is, no doubt, a difficult question, and one about which the best Christians are not entirely of one mind. The plain truth is that inspiration is *a miracle*, and, like all miracles, there is much about it which we cannot fully understand.

We must not confound it with intellectual power, such as great poets and authors possess. To talk of Shakespeare and Milton and Byron being inspired, like Moses and St Paul, is to my mind almost profane.

Nor must we confound it with the gifts and graces bestowed on the early Christians in the primitive Church. All the Apostles were enabled to preach and to work miracles, but not all were inspired to write.

We must rather regard it as a special supernatural gift, bestowed on about thirty people out of mankind, in order to qualify them for the special business of writing the Scriptures; and we must be content to allow that, like everything miraculous, we cannot entirely explain it, though we can believe it. A miracle would not be a miracle if it could be explained. That miracles are possible, I do not stop to prove here. I never trouble myself on that subject until those who deny miracles have fairly grappled with the great fact that Christ rose again from the dead.

I firmly believe that miracles are possible, and have been wrought; and among great miracles I place the fact that men were inspired by God to write the Bible. Inspiration, therefore, being a miracle, I frankly allow that there are difficulties about it which at present I cannot fully solve.

The exact manner in which the minds of the inspired writers of Scripture worked when they wrote, I do not pretend to explain. Very likely they could not have explained it themselves. I do not admit for a moment that they were mere machines holding pens, and, like type-setters in a printing-office, did not understand what they were doing. I abhor the 'mechanical' theory of inspiration. I dislike the idea that men like Moses and St Paul were no better than organ pipes, employed by the Holy Ghost, or ignorant secretaries or amanuenses who wrote by dictation what they did not understand. I admit nothing of the kind.

I believe that in some marvellous manner the Holy Ghost made use of the reason, the memory, the intellect, the style of thought, and the peculiar mental temperament of each writer of the Scriptures. But how and in what manner this was done I can no more explain than I can the union of two natures, God and man, in the person of our blessed Lord Jesus Christ. I only know that there is both a divine and a human element in the Bible and that, while the men who wrote it were really and truly men, the book that they wrote and handed down to us is really and truly the Word of God. I know the *result*, but I do not understand the *process*.

The result is that the Bible is the written Word of God but I can no more explain the process than I can explain how the water became wine at Cana, or how five loaves fed five thousand men, or how a word raised Lazarus from the dead. I do not pretend to explain miracles, and I do not pretend to explain fully the miraculous gift of inspiration. The position I take up is that, while the Bible-writers were not 'machines', as some sneeringly say, they only wrote what God taught them to write. The Holy Ghost put into their minds thoughts and ideas, and then guided their pens in writing them. When you read the Bible you are not reading the unaided, self-taught composition of erring men like ourselves, but thoughts and words which were suggested by the eternal God. The men who were employed to indite the Scripture spake not of themselves. They 'spake as they were moved by the Holy Ghost' (*2 Pet.* 1:21.) He that holds a Bible in his hand should know that he holds 'not the word of men, but . . . of God' (*1 Thess.* 2:13).

Inspiration Is Verbal

Concerning the precise extent to which the Bible is inspired, I freely admit that Christians differ widely. Some of the views put forth on the subject appear to me to be erroneous in the extreme. I shall not shrink from giving my own opinion and stating my reasons for maintaining it. In matters like these I dare not call any man master. Painful as it is to disagree with able and gifted men on religious questions, I dare not take up views of inspiration which my head and heart tell me are unsound, however high and honoured the names of those who maintain them. I believe in my conscience that low and defective views of the subject are doing immense damage to the cause of Christ in these last days.

Some hold that some of the books of Scripture are not inspired at all, and have no more authority or claim to our reverence than the writings of any ordinary man.

Others who do not go so far as this, and allow that all the books in the Bible are inspired, maintain that inspiration was only partial, and that there are portions in almost every book which are uninspired.

Others hold that inspiration means nothing more than general superintendence and direction, and that, while the Bible writers were miraculously preserved from making mistakes in great things and matters necessary to salvation, in things indifferent they were left to their own unassisted faculties, like any other writers.

Some hold that all the ideas in the Bible were given by inspiration, but not the words and language in which they are clothed; though how to separate ideas from words, it is rather hard to understand!

Some, finally, allow the thorough inspiration of all the Bible, and yet maintain that it was possible for the writers to make occasional mistakes in their statements, and that such mistakes do exist at this day.

From all these views I totally and entirely dissent. They all appear to me more or less defective, below the truth, dangerous in their tendency, and open to grave and insuperable objections. The view which I maintain is that *every book, and chapter, and verse, and syllable of the Bible was originally given by inspiration of God.*

I hold that not only the substance of the Bible, but its language, not only the ideas of the Bible, but its words, not only certain parts of the Bible, but every chapter of the book, that all and each are of divine authority. I hold that the Scripture not only *contains* the Word of God, but *is* the Word of God. I believe the narratives and statements of Genesis, and the catalogues in Chronicles, were just as truly written by inspiration as the Acts of the Apostles. I believe Ezra's account of the nine-and-twenty knives, and St Paul's message about the cloak and parchments, were as much written under divine direction as the 20th chapter of Exodus, the 17th of John, or the 8th of Romans.

I do not say, be it remembered, that all these parts of the Bible are of equal importance to our souls. Nothing of the kind! But I do say they were all equally given by inspiration.[1]

In making this statement I ask the reader not to misunderstand my meaning. I do not forget that the Old Testament was written in Hebrew and the New Testament in Greek. The inspiration of every word, for which I contend, is the inspiration of every original Hebrew and Greek word, as the Bible writers first wrote it down. I stand up

---

[1] 'We affirm that the Bible is the Word of God, and that it is not marred with human infirmities. We do not imagine, with some, that the Bible is like a threshing-floor, on which wheat and chaff lie mingled together, and that it is left for the reader to winnow and sift the wheat from the chaff by the fan and sieve of his own mind' (Wordsworth on *Inspiration*, p. 11).

for nothing more and nothing less than this. I lay no claim to the inspiration of every word in the various versions and translations of God's Word.

So far as those translations and versions are faithfully and correctly done, so far they are of equal authority with the original Hebrew and Greek. We have reason to thank God that many of the translations are, in the main, faithful and accurate. At any rate our own English Bible, if not perfect, is so far correct, that in reading it we have a right to believe that we are reading in our own tongue not the word of man, but the Word of God.

Now the view for which I contend, that every word of the Bible is inspired, is not accepted by many good Christians, and is bitterly opposed in many quarters. I shall therefore mention a few reasons why it appears to me the only safe and tenable view which can be adopted, and the only one which is free from innumerable objections.

If I err in maintaining it I have the comfort, at any rate, of erring in good company. I only take up the same ground which almost all the Fathers occupied; which Bishop Jewell, and Hooker, and Owen, took up long ago; and which Chalmers, Robert Haldane, Gaussen, Bishop Wordsworth, M'Caul, Burgon, and Archdeacon Lee of the Irish Church, have ably defended in modern days.

I know, however, that men's minds are variously consti-tuted. Arguments and reasons which appear weighty to some are of no weight with others. I shall content myself with setting down in order the reasons which satisfy me.

Verbal Inspiration Defended: 1. The Bible as a Perfect Rule

For one thing I cannot see *how the Bible can be a perfect rule of faith and practice* if it is not fully inspired, and if it contains any flaws and imperfections. If the Bible is anything at all it is the statute-book of God's kingdom, the code of laws and regulations by which the subjects of that kingdom are to live, the register-deed of the terms on which they have peace now and shall have glory hereafter.

Now, why are we to suppose that such a book will be loosely and imperfectly drawn up, any more than legal deeds drawn up on earth? Every lawyer can tell us that in legal deeds and statutes every word is of importance, and that property, life, or death, may often turn on a single word. Think of the confusion that would ensue if wills, and settlements, and conveyances, and partnership-deeds, and leases, and agreements, and acts of parliament were not carefully drawn up and carefully interpreted, and every word allowed its due weight.

Where would be the use of such documents if particular words went for nothing, and every one had a right to add, or take away, or alter, or deny the validity of words, or erase words at his own discretion? At this rate we might as well lay aside our legal documents altogether. Surely we have a right to expect that in the book which contains our title-deeds for eternity every word will be inspired, and nothing imperfect admitted. If God's statute-book is not inspired, and every word is not of divine authority, God's subjects are left in a pitiable state. I see much in this.

2. The Bible's Own Claims

For another thing, if the Bible is not fully inspired and contains imperfections, I cannot understand the language which is frequently used about it in its own pages. Such expressions as 'The oracles of God'; 'He saith'; 'God saith'; 'the Holy Ghost spake by Esaias the prophet'; 'the Holy Ghost saith, "To-day if ye will hear His voice"', would appear to me inexplicable and extravagant if applied to a book containing occasional blemishes, defects, and mistakes (*Acts* 7:38; *Rom.* 3:2; *Heb.* 5:12; *1 Pet.* 4:11; *Eph.* 4:8; *Heb.* 1:8; *Acts* 28:25; *Heb.* 3:7; *Heb.* 10:15; *Rom.* 9:25).

Once grant that every word of Scripture is inspired, and I see an admirable propriety in the language. I cannot understand 'the Holy Ghost' making a mistake, or an 'oracle' containing anything defective! If any man replies that the Holy Ghost did not always speak by Isaiah, I will ask him, Who is to decide when He did and when He did not? I see much in this.

3. Arguments Turning on the Precise Wording

For another thing, the theory that the Bible was not given by inspiration of God appears to me utterly at variance with several quotations from the Old Testament which I find in the New. I allude to those quotations in which *the whole force of the passage turns on one single word*, and once even on the use of the singular instead of the plural number.

Take, for instance, such quotations as, 'The LORD said unto my Lord' (*Matt.* 22:44); 'I said, Ye are gods' (*John* 10:34); 'To Abraham and his seed were the promises made. He saith not, And to seeds, as of many; but as of one, And to thy seed, which is Christ' (*Gal.* 3:16); 'He is not ashamed to call them brethren, saying, I will declare Thy name unto my brethren' (*Heb.* 2:11–12). In every one of these cases the whole point of the quotation lies in a single word.

It would be easy to multiply texts in proof of this point. I will only name the following: *Heb.* 2:8; 3:7–19; 4:2–11; 12:27.

But if this is so, it is hard to see on what principle we can deny the inspiration of *all* the words of Scripture. At any rate, those who deny verbal inspiration will find it difficult to show us which words are inspired and which are not. Who is to draw the line, and where is it to be drawn? I see much in this.

4. The Bible as a Weapon in Controversy

For another thing, if the words of Scripture are not all inspired, the value of the Bible as a weapon in controversy is greatly damaged, if not entirely taken away.

Who does not know that in arguing with Jews, Arians, or Socinians, the whole point of the texts we quote against them often lies in a single word? What are we to reply if an adversary asserts that the special word of some text, on which we ground an argument, is a mistake of the writer, and therefore of no authority? To my mind it appears that the objection would be fatal. It is useless to quote texts if we once admit that not all the words of which they are composed were given by inspiration.

Unless there is some certain standard to appeal to we may as well hold our tongues. Argument is labour in vain if our mouths are to be stopped by the retort, 'That text is not inspired.' I see much in this.

5. The Bible as a Means of Instruction

For another thing, to give up verbal inspiration appears to me to destroy the usefulness of the Bible as an instrument of public preaching and instruction.

Where is the use of choosing a text and making it the subject of a pulpit address, if we do not believe that every word of the text is inspired? Once let our hearers get hold of the idea that the writers of the Bible could make mistakes in the particular words they used, and they will care little for any reproofs, or exhortations, or remarks which are based on words.

'How do you know', they might ask us, 'that this word, about which you made such ado yesterday, was given by the Holy Ghost? How do you know that St Paul, or St Peter, or St John did not make a mistake, and use the wrong word? That they could make mistakes about words you yourself allow.'

I know not what others may think. For myself, I could give no answer. I see much in this.

6. The Bible as a Source of Comfort

Last, but not least, the denial of verbal inspiration appears to me to destroy a great part of the usefulness of the Bible as a source of comfort and instruction in private reading.

Where is the true Christian student of the Bible who does not know that words, particular words, afford a large portion of the benefit which he derives from his daily reading? How much the value of many a cherished text depends on some single phrase, or the number of a substantive, or the tense of a verb? Alas! there would be an end of all this if we once concede that each word is not inspired; and that, for anything we know, some much-loved favourite substantive, or verb, or pronoun, or adverb, or adjective, was an Apostle's mistake, and the word of man, not of God!

What others might think I know not. For myself, I should be tempted to lay aside my Bible in despair, and become of all men most miserable. I see much in this.

4

Objections Answered

Now I freely grant that many excellent Christians think that the view I maintain is open to serious objections. That the Bible, generally speaking, is given by inspiration, they firmly maintain. But they shrink from maintaining that inspiration extends to every word of Scripture.

I am sorry to differ from these worthy people. But I cannot see the weight and force of their objections. Fairly and honestly examined, they fail to carry conviction to my mind.

1. Alleged Historical Errors

Some object that there are occasional statements in the Bible which contradict the facts of history. Are these all verbally inspired? My answer is that it is far more easy to assert this than to prove it. There is nothing of which we have so few trustworthy remains as very ancient history, and if ancient uninspired history and Bible history seem to disagree, it is generally safer and wiser to believe that Bible history is right and other history wrong.

At any rate, it is a singular fact that all recent researches in Assyria, Babylon, Palestine, and Egypt, show an extraordinary tendency to confirm the perfect accuracy of the Word of God. The lamented Mr Smith's discoveries at Babylon are a remarkable example of what I mean. There are buried evidences which God seems to keep in reserve for these last days. If Bible history and other histories cannot be made to agree at present, it is safest to wait.

2. Alleged Scientific Errors

Some object that there are occasional statements in the Bible which contradict the facts of natural science. Are these all inspired? My answer is, again, that it is far more easy to assert this than to prove it.

The Bible was not written to teach a system of geology, botany, or astronomy, or a history of birds, insects, and animals, and on matters touching these subjects it wisely uses popular language, such as common people can understand. No one thinks of saying that the Astronomer Royal contradicts science because he speaks of the sun's 'rising and setting'. If the Bible said anywhere that the earth was a flat surface, or that it was a fixed globe round which the sun revolved, or that it never existed in any state before Adam and Eve, there might be something in the objection. But it never does so. It speaks of scientific subjects as they appear. But it never flatly contradicts science.[1]

3. 'Unbelievable' Statements

Some object that there are occasional statements in the Bible which are monstrous, absurd, and incredible. Are they really obliged to believe that Eve was tempted by the devil in the form of a serpent, that Noah was saved in an ark, that the Israelites crossed the Red Sea between two walls of water, that Balaam's ass spoke, and that Jonah actually went into the whale's belly? Are all these statements inspired?

My answer is that Christ's apostles speak of these things as historical facts, and were more likely to know the truth about them than we are. After all, do we believe in

[1]'The language of Scripture is necessarily adapted to the common state of man's intellectual development, in which he is not supposed to be possessed of science. Hence the phrases used by Scripture are precisely those which science soon teaches man to consider inaccurate. Yet they are not on that account the less fitted for their purpose, for if any terms had been used adapted to a more advanced state of knowledge, they must have been unintelligible to those to whom the Scripture was first addressed' (Whewell's *Philosophy of Inductive Science*. Vol. 1, p. 686).

miracles or not? Do we believe that Christ Himself rose from the dead?

Let us stick to that one grand miracle first, and disprove it if we can. If we do believe it, it is foolish to object to things because they are miraculous.

4. Supposedly Trivial Statements

Some object that there are things mentioned occasionally in the Bible which are so trifling that they are unworthy to be called inspired. They point to St Paul's writing about his cloak, and books, and parchments, and ask if we really think that the Apostle wrote about such little matters by inspiration of God?

I answer that the least things affecting any of God's children are not too small for the notice of Him who 'numbers the hairs of our heads'. There are excellent and edifying lessons to be learned from the cloak and the parchments, as Robert Haldane has shown most convincingly, in his work on *The Evidences of Divine Revelation*.

After all, man knows very little what is great and what is small in God's sight. The history of Nimrod 'the mighty hunter' is dispatched in three verses of Genesis, and the history of a Syrian dwelling in tents, called Abraham, fills up no less than fourteen chapters.

The microscope applied to the book of nature, can show us God's hand in the least lichen that grows on the top of

Scafell as well as in the cedar of Lebanon. The veriest trifles, as they seem to us, in the Book of Scripture, may turn out to be most striking confirmations of its truth. Paley has shown this admirably in his *Horae Paulinae*, and Professor Blunt in his *Undesigned Coincidences*.

5. Alleged Discrepancies

Some object that there are grave discrepancies in some of the Bible histories, especially in the four Gospels, which cannot be made to harmonize and agree. Are the words, they ask, all inspired in these cases? Have the writers made no mistakes?

I answer that the number of these discrepancies is grossly exaggerated, and that in many cases they are only apparent, and disappear under the touch of common sense. Even in the hardest of them we should remember, in common fairness, that circumstances are very likely kept back from us which entirely reconcile everything, if we only knew them.

Very often in these days when two honest, veracious men give a separate account of some long story their accounts do not quite tally because one dwells on one part and the other on another. All well-informed students of history know that the precise day when Charles I erected his standard at Nottingham, in the Parliamentary war, has not been settled to this hour.

6. Inspired Records of Uninspired Speeches

Some object that Job's friends, in their long speeches, said many weak and foolish things. Were all their words inspired?

An objection like this arises from an illogical and confused idea of what inspiration means. The book of Job contains an historical account of a wonderful part of the old patriarch's history, and a report both of his speeches and of those of his friends. But we are nowhere told that either Job or Eliphaz and his companions spoke all that they spoke by the Holy Ghost. The writer of the book of Job was thoroughly inspired to record all they said. But whether they spoke rightly or wrongly is to be decided by the general teaching of Scripture.

No one would say that St Peter was inspired when he said, 'I know not the Man,' in the High Priest's palace. But the writer of the Gospel was inspired when he wrote it down for our learning.

In the Acts of the Apostles the letter of Claudius Lysias was certainly not written by inspiration, and Gamaliel, and the town clerk of Ephesus, and Tertullus, were not inspired when they made their speeches. But it is equally certain that St Luke was inspired to write them down and record them in his book.

7. Does Paul Disclaim Inspiration?

Some object that St Paul, in 1 Corinthians, chapter 7, when giving certain advice to the Corinthian Church, says at one time, 'Not I, but the Lord', and at another, 'I, not the Lord'. And they ask, Does not this show that in part of his advice he was not inspired?

I answer, Not at all. A careful study of the chapter will show that when the Apostle says 'Not I, but the Lord', he lays down some principles on which the Lord had spoken already; and when he says 'I, not the Lord', he gives advice on some point about which there bad been no revelation hitherto. But there is not the slightest proof that he is not writing all the way through under direct inspiration of God.

8. Various Readings

Some object that there are many various readings of the words of Scripture, and that we cannot, therefore, feel sure that we have the original inspired Word of God.

I answer that the various readings, when fairly examined, will prove to be absurdly exaggerated in number and importance. Dr Kennicott, Bengel, and others have proved this long ago. No doubt we may have lost a few of the original words. We have no right to expect infallibility in transcribers and copyists, before the invention of printing. But there is not a single doctrine in Scripture which would be affected or altered if all the various readings were allowed, and all the disputed or doubtful words were omitted.

Considering how many hands the Bible passed through before printing was invented, and who the transcribers were, it is marvellous that the various readings are so few!

The fact that about the immense majority of all the words in the old Hebrew and Greek Scriptures there is no doubt at all, is little short of a miracle, and demands much thanksgiving to God.

One thing is very certain. There is no ancient book which has been handed down to us with so good a text and so few various readings as the Bible.

9. Extracts from Uninspired Records

Finally, some object that occasional parts of the Bible are taken out, copied, and extracted from the writings of uninspired men, such as historical chronicles, and pedigrees, and lists of names. Are all these to be regarded as inspired?

I reply that there seems no reason why the Holy Ghost should not have directed the Bible writers to use materials made ready to their hands, as well as facts which they had seen themselves, and, by so directing them, have invested such words as they used with divine authority. When

St Paul quoted lines from heathen poets he did not mean us to regard them as inspired. But he was taught by God to clothe his ideas in the words which they had used, and by so doing he very likely obtained a favourable hearing from many. And when we read such quotations, or read lists of names taken from Jewish chronicles and registers, we need not doubt that the Bible writers were taught to use such materials by inspiration of God.

* * * * *

I leave the objections to verbal inspiration at this point, and will detain my readers no longer with them. I will not pretend to deny that the subject has its difficulties, which will probably never be completely solved.

I cannot perhaps clear up such difficulties as the mention of 'Jeremy the prophet' in Matthew 27, or reconcile the third and sixth hour in St John's and St. Mark's accounts of the crucifixion, or explain Stephen's account of Jacob's burial in the seventh chapter of Acts, to my own entire satisfaction. But I have no doubt these difficulties can be explained, and perhaps will be some day.

These things do not move me. I expect difficulties in such a deep and miraculous matter as inspiration, which I have not eyes to see through. I am content to wait. It was a wise saying of Faraday that 'there are many questions about which it is the highest philosophy to keep our minds in a state of judicious suspense'. It should be a settled rule with us never to give up a great principle, when we have got hold of it, on account of difficulties. Time often makes things clear which at first look dark.

The view of inspiration which presents to my own mind the fewest difficulties is that in which all the words of Scripture, as well as the thoughts, are regarded as inspired. Here I take my stand.

Remember what I have just said. Never give up a great principle in theology on account of difficulties. Wait patiently, and the difficulties may all melt away. Let that be an axiom in your mind. Suffer me to mention an illustration of what I mean. Persons who are conversant with astronomy know that before the discovery of the planet Neptune there were difficulties which greatly troubled the most scientific astronomers respecting certain aberrations of the planet Uranus. These aberrations puzzled the minds of astronomers; and some of them suggested that they might possibly prove the whole Newtonian system to be untrue.

But just at that time a well-known French astronomer, named Leverrier, read before the Academy of Science at Paris a paper in which he laid down this great axiom, that it did not become a scientific man to give up a principle because of difficulties which apparently could not be explained. He said in effect, 'We cannot explain the aberrations of Uranus now; but we may be sure that the Newtonian system will be proved to be right, sooner or later. Something may be discovered one day which will prove that these aberrations may be accounted for, and yet the Newtonian system remain true and unshaken.'

A few years after, the anxious eyes of astronomers discovered the last great planet, Neptune. This planet was shown to be the true cause of all the aberrations of Uranus; and what the French astronomer had laid down as a principle in science was proved to be wise and true. The application of the anecdote is obvious. Let us beware of giving up any first principle in theology. Let us not give up the great principle of plenary verbal inspiration because of apparent difficulties. The day may come when they will all be solved.

In the meantime we may rest assured that the difficulties which beset any other theory of inspiration are tenfold greater than any which beset our own.

5

Conclusion

Let me now conclude this paper with a few words of plain application. Let us lay aside all deep discussion of hard things about the manner of inspiration. Let us take it for granted that, in some way or other, whether we can explain it or not, we hold the Bible to be the Word of God. Let us start from this point. Let my readers give me a hearing, while I say a few things which appear to me to deserve their attention.

1. Do Not Neglect the Bible

Is the Bible the Word of God? Then mind *that you do not neglect it*. Read it, read it! Begin to read it this very day. What greater insult to God can a man be guilty of than to refuse to read the letter God sends him from heaven? Oh, be sure, if you will not read your Bible, you are in fearful danger of losing your soul!

You are in danger, *because God will reckon with you for your neglect of the Bible in the day of judgment.* You will have to give account of your use of time, strength, and money; and you will also have to give account of your use of the Word. You will not stand at that bar on the same level, in point of responsibility, with the dweller in central Africa, who never heard of the Bible. Oh, no! To whom much is given, of them much will be required. Of all men's buried talents, none will weigh them down so heavily as a neglected Bible. As you deal with the Bible, so God will deal with your soul. Will you not repent, and turn over a new leaf in life, and read your Bible?

You are in danger, *because there is no degree of error in religion into which you may not fall.* You are at the mercy of the first clever Jesuit, Mormon, Socinian, Turk, or Jew, who may happen to meet you. A land of unwalled villages is not more defenceless against an enemy than a man who neglects his Bible. You may go on tumbling from one step of delusion to another, till at length you are landed in the pit of hell. I say once more, Will you not repent and read your Bible?

You are in danger, *because there is not a single reasonable excuse you can allege for neglecting the Bible.* You have no time to read it, forsooth! But you can make time for eating, drinking, sleeping, getting money and spending money, and perhaps for newspaper reading and smoking. You might easily make time to read the Word. Alas, it is not want of time, but waste of time that ruins souls! You find it too troublesome to read, forsooth! You had better say at once it is too much trouble to go to heaven, and you are content to go to hell. Truly these excuses are like the rubbish round the walls of Jerusalem in Nehemiah's days. They would all soon disappear if, like the Jews, you had 'a mind to work'. I say for the last time, Will you not repent and read your Bible?

Believe me, believe me, the Bible itself is the best witness of its own inspiration. The men who quibble and make difficulties about inspiration are too often the very men who never read the Scriptures at all. The darkness and hardness and obscurity they profess to complain of are far more often in their own hearts than in the book. Oh, be persuaded! Take it up and begin to read.

2. Read the Bible Reverently

Is the Bible the Word of God? Then be sure you always *read it with deep reverence*. Say to your soul, whenever you open the Bible, 'O my soul, thou art going to read a message from God.'

The sentences of judges, and the speeches of kings, are received with awe and respect. How much more reverence is due to the words of the Judge of judges and King of kings! Avoid, as you would cursing and swearing, that irreverent habit of mind into which some modern divines have unhappily fallen, in speaking about the Bible. They handle the contents of the holy book as carelessly and disrespectfully as if the writers were such men as themselves.

They make one think of a child composing a book to expose the fancied ignorance of his own father, or of a pardoned murderer criticizing the handwriting and style of his own reprieve. Enter rather into the spirit of Moses on Mount Horeb: 'Put thy shoes from off thy feet; the place whereon thou standest is holy ground.'

3. Read the Bible with Fervent Prayer

Is the Bible the Word of God? Then be sure you *never read it without fervent prayer* for the help and teaching of the Holy Spirit.

Here is the rock on which many make shipwreck. They do not ask for wisdom and instruction, and so they find the Bible dark, and carry nothing away from it. You should pray for the Spirit to guide you into all truth. You should beg the Lord Jesus Christ to 'open your understanding,' as He did that of His disciples. The Lord God, by whose inspiration the book was written, keeps the keys of the book, and alone can enable you to understand it profitably. Nine times over in one Psalm does David cry, 'Teach me.' Five times over, in the same Psalm, does he say, 'Give me understanding.' Well says John Owen, Dean of Christ Church, Oxford, 'There is a sacred light in the Word: but there is a covering and veil on the eyes of men, so that they cannot behold it aright. Now, the removal of this veil is the peculiar work of the Holy Spirit.' Humble prayer will throw more light on your Bible than Poole, or Henry, or Scott, or Burkitt, or Bengel, or Alford, or Wordsworth, or Barnes, or Ellicott, or Lightfoot, or any commentary that ever was written.

The Bible is a large book or a small one, a dark or a bright one, according to the spirit in which men read it. Intellect alone will do nothing with it. Wranglers and first-class men will not understand it unless their hearts are right as well as their heads.

The highest critical and grammatical knowledge will find it a sealed book without the teaching of the Holy Ghost. Its contents are often 'hid to the wise and prudent and revealed to babes'. Remember this, and say always, when you open your Bible, 'O God, for Christ's sake, give me the teaching of the Spirit.'

4. Prize the Bible More

Finally, is the Bible the Word of God? Then let us all resolve from this day forward, to *prize the Bible more*. Let us not fear being idolaters of this blessed book.

Men may easily make an idol of the Church, of ministers, of sacraments, or of intellect. Men cannot make an idol of the Word. Let us regard all who would damage the authority of the Bible, or impugn its credit, as spiritual robbers.

We are travelling through a wilderness: they rob us of our only guide. We are voyaging over a stormy sea: they rob us of our only compass. We are toiling over a weary road: they pluck our staff out of our hands. And what do these spiritual robbers give us in place of the Bible? What do they offer as a safer guide and better provision for our souls? Nothing! absolutely nothing! Big swelling words! Empty promises of new light! High sounding jargon; but nothing substantial and real! They would fain take from us the bread of life, and they do not give us in its place so much as a stone. Let us turn a deaf ear to them. Let us firmly grasp and prize the Bible more and more, the more it is assaulted.

Let us hear the conclusion of the whole matter. God has given us the Bible to be a light to guide us to everlasting life. Let us not neglect this precious gift. Let us read it diligently, walk in its light, and we shall be saved.

Appendix 1:

Quotations on the Inspiration of the Bible

The following quotations about inspiration, from the works of four eminent British theologians, I venture to think deserve attentive perusal. They are valuable in themselves on account of the arguments which they contain. They also supply abundant proof that the high view of verbal inspiration which I advocate in this paper is no modern invention, but an 'old path' in which many of God's ablest children have walked, and found it a good way.

1. Bishop Jewell

Bishop Jewell, the author of the Apology, *was unquestionably one of the most learned of the English Reformers. Let us hear what he says:*

'St Paul, speaking of the Word of God, saith, "The whole Scripture is given by inspiration of God, and is profitable." Many think the Apostle's speech is hardly true of the whole Scripture, that all and every part of the Scripture is profitable. Much is spoken of genealogies and pedigrees, of lepers, of sacrificing goats and oxen, etc. These seem to have little profit in them: to be idle and vain.

'If they show vain in thine eyes, yet hath not the Lord set them down in vain. The words of the Lord are pure words, as the silver tried in a furnace of earth refined seven times. There is no sentence, no clause, no word, no syllable, no letter, but it is written for thy instruction: there is not one jot but it is sealed and signed with the blood of the Lamb.

'Our imaginations are idle, our thoughts are vain: there is no idleness, no vanity, in the Word of God.

'Those oxen and goats which were sacrificed teach thee to kill the uncleanness and filthiness of thine heart: they teach thee that thou art guilty of death, when thy life must be redeemed by the death of some beast: they lead thee to believe the forgiveness of sins by a more perfect sacrifice, since it was not possible that the blood of bulls or of goats should take away sins.

'That leprosy teacheth thee the uncleanness and leprosy of thy soul.

'These genealogies and pedigrees lead us to the birth of our Saviour Christ, so that the whole Word of God is pure and holy. No word, no letter, no syllable, nor point or prick thereof, but is written and preserved for thy sake.'

Jewell on *The Holy Scriptures.*

2. RICHARD HOOKER

Richard Hooker, author of the Ecclesiastical Polity, *is justly respected by all schools of thought in the Church of England as 'the judicious Hooker'. Let us hear what he says:*

'Touching the manner how men, by the Spirit of Prophecy in Holy Scripture, have spoken and written of things to come, we must understand, that as the knowledge of that they spake, so likewise the utterance of that they knew, came not by those usual and ordinary means whereby we are brought to understand the mysteries of our salvation, and are wont to instruct others in the same. For whatsoever we know, we have it by the hands and ministry of men, who led us along like children from a letter to a syllable, from a syllable to a word, from a word to a line, from a line to a sentence from a sentence to a side, and so turn over.

'But God Himself was their instructor. He Himself taught them, partly by dreams and visions in the night, partly by revelations in the day, taking them aside from amongst their brethren, and talking with them as a man would talk with his neighbours in the way. Thus they became acquainted even with the secret and hidden counsels of God; they saw things which themselves were not able to utter, they beheld that whereat men and angels are astonished, they understood in the beginning what should come to pass in the last days. God who lightened thus the eyes of their understanding, giving them knowledge by unusual and extraordinary means, *did also miraculously Himself frame and fashion their words and writings,* in so much that a greater difference there seemeth not to be between the manner of their knowledge, than there is between the manner of their speech and ours. "We have received", saith the Apostle, "not the spirit of the world, but the Spirit which is of God, that we might know the things that are given to us of God: which things also we speak, not in words which man's wisdom teacheth, but which the Holy Ghost doth teach."

'This is that which the Prophets mean by those books written full within and without; which books were so often delivered them to eat, not because God fed them with ink and paper, but to teach us, that so often as He employed them in this heavenly work, *they neither spake nor wrote any word of their own, but uttered syllable by syllable as the Spirit put it in their mouths,* no otherwise than the harp or the lute doth give a sound according to the direction of his hands that holdeth it and striketh it with skill.'

Hooker's *Works,* vol. 3, pp. 537, 540.

3. JOHN OWEN

John Owen, Dean of Christ Church, Oxford, was the most learned and argumentative of the Puritans. Let us hear what he says:

'Holy men of God spake as they were moved by the Holy Ghost. When the word was thus brought to them it was not left to their own understandings, wisdom, minds, memories, to order, dispose, and give it out; but they were borne, actuated, carried out by the Holy Ghost, to speak, deliver, and write all that, and nothing but that, to very tittles, that was so brought unto them. They invented not words themselves, suited to the things they had learned, but only expressed the word that they received. Though their mind and understanding were used in the choice of words (whence arise all the differences in their manner of expression), yet they were so guided that their words were not their own, but immediately supplied unto them. Not only the doctrine they taught was the word of truth, truth itself, but the words whereby they taught it were words of truth from God Himself.

'Thus, allowing the contribution of proper instruments for the reception and representation of words which answer to the mind and tongue of the Prophets in the coming of the voice of God to them, every apex of the written Word is equally divine, and as immediately from

God as the voice wherewith, or whereby, He spake to us in the Prophets; and is therefore accompanied with the same authority in itself and to us.'

The Divine Original of the Scripture, Works, vol. 16,
p. 305.

4. THOMAS CHALMERS

Dr Chalmers was probably the most intellectual and deep-thinking theologian that intellectual Scotland has ever produced. Let us hear what he says:

1. 'The subject-matter of the Bible had to pass through the minds of the selected Prophets and Apostles, and to issue thence in language ere it comes forth in the shape of Scripture upon the world. Now it is here that we meet the advocates of a *partial* or mitigated inspiration, and would make common cause *against one and all of them.*

'There is not one theory short, by however so little, of a thorough and perfect inspiration, there is not one of them but is chargeable with the consequence, that the subject-matter of revelation suffers and is deteriorated in the closing footsteps of its progress; and just before it settles into that ultimate position, where it stands forth to guide and illuminate the world. It existed purely in heaven. It descended purely from heaven to earth. It was deposited purely by the great Agent of revelation in the minds of the Apostles. But then we are told that when but a little way from the final landing place, then, instead of being carried forward purely to the situation where alone the great purpose of the whole movement was to be fulfilled, then was it abandoned to itself, and then were human infirmities permitted to mingle with it, and to mar its lustre.

'Strange, that just when entering on the functions of an authoritative guide and leader to mankind, that then, and not till then, the soil and the feebleness of humanity should be suffered to gather around it. Strange, that, with the inspiration of thoughts, it should make pure ingress into the minds of the Apostles; but wanting the inspiration of words should not make pure egress to that world in whose behalf alone, and for whose admonition alone, this great movement originated in heaven, and terminated in earth.

'Strange, more especially strange, in the face of the declaration that not unto themselves but unto us they ministered these things, strange, nevertheless, that this revelation should come in purely to themselves, but to us should come forth impurely, with somewhat, it would appear, with somewhat the taint and the obscuration of human frailty attached to it.

'It matters not at what point in the progress of this celestial truth to our world the obscuration has been cast upon it. It comes to us a dim and desecrated thing at last; and man instead of holding converse with God's unspotted testimony, has an imperfect, a mutilated Bible put into his hands.'

[60]

2. 'Such being our views, it is the unavoidable consequence of them that we should hold the Bible, for all the purposes of a revelation, to be perfect in its language, as well as perfect in its doctrine. And for this conclusion it is not necessary that we should arbitrate between the theories of superintendence and suggestion. The superintendence that would barely intercept the progress of error, we altogether discard, conceiving, that, if this term be applicable to the process of inspiration at all, it must be that efficient superintendence which not only secures that, negatively, there shall be nothing wrong, but which also secures that, affirmatively, there should at all times have emanated from the sacred penmen, the fittest topics, and these couched in the fittest and most appropriate expression. Whether this has been effected partly by superintendence and partly by suggestion, or wholly by suggestion, we care not. We have no inclination and no taste for these distinctions.

'Our cause is independent of them; nor can we fully participate in the fears of those alarmists who think that our cause is materially injured by them. The important question with us is not the *process* of the manufacture, but the *qualities* of the resulting commodity. The former we hold not to be a relevant, and we are not sure that it is a legitimate inquiry. It is on the latter we take our stand; and the superabundant testimonies of Scripture on the worth and the perfection and the absolute authority of the Word

– these form the strong-holds of an argument that goes to establish all which the most rigid advocates for a *total and infallible inspiration* ought to desire.

'Our concern is with the work, and not with the workmanship; nor need we intrude into the mysteries of the hidden operation, if only assured by the explicit testimonies of Scripture that the product of that operation, is, both in substance and expression, a perfect directory of faith and practice. We believe that, in the composition of that record, men not only thought as they were inspired, but spake as they were moved by the Holy Ghost.

'But our argument for the absolute perfection of Holy Writ is invulnerably beyond the reach even of those who have attempted to trace with geographical precision the line which separates the miraculous from the natural; and tell us when it was that Apostles wrote the words which the Spirit prompted them, and when it was that they wrote the words which the Spirit permitted them. To the result, in our humble apprehension, it positively matters not. Did they speak the words that the Spirit prompted, these words were therefore the best. Did they speak the words which the Spirit permitted, it was because these words were the best. *The optimism of the Bible is alike secured in both these ways;* and the sanction of the Spirit extended, both in respect of sentiments and of sayings, *to every clause* of it. In either way, they effectively are the words of the Spirit; and God through the Bible is not presenting truths through the medium of others' language. He in effect has made it His own language; and God, through the Bible, is speaking to us.'

3. 'It is the part of Christians to rise like a wall of fire around the integrity and inspiration of Scripture; and to hold them as intact and inviolable as if a rampart were thrown around them whose foundations are on earth and whose battlements are in heaven. It is this tampering with limits that destroys and defaces everything; and therefore it is precisely when the limit is broken that the alarm should be sounded. If the battle-cry is to be lifted at all, it should be lifted at the outset; and so on the first mingling, by however so slight an infusion, of things human with things divine, all the friends of the Bible should join heart and hand against so foul and fearful a desecration.'

Chalmers' *Christian Evidences*, vol. 2, pp. 371, 372, 375, 376, 396.

Appendix 2:

'Not Corrupting the Word'

'For we are not as many, which corrupt the word
of God: but as of sincerity, but as of God, in the
sight of God speak we in Christ'
(*2 Cor.* 2:17).

I
t is no light matter to speak to any assembly of immortal souls about the things of God. But the most serious of all responsibilities is to speak to a gathering of ministers, such as that which I now see before me. The awful feeling will come across my mind, that one single word said wrong, sinking into some heart, and bearing fruit at some future

---

[1] An address given by J. C. Ryle at an aggregate Clerical Meeting in Weston-super-Mare, August 1858, previously published in *Warnings to the Churches* (ISBN 0 85151 0434, 176 pp., pbk).

time, in some pulpit, may lead to harm, of which we cannot know the extent.

But there are occasions when true humility is to be seen, not so much in loud professions of our weakness, as in forgetting ourselves altogether. I desire to forget self at this time, in turning my attention to this portion of Scripture. If I say little about my own sense of insufficiency, do me the justice to believe that it is not because I do not feel it much.

The Greek expression which we have translated, 'corrupt', is derived from a word, the etymology of which is not quite agreed on by lexicographers. It either means a tradesman, who does his business dishonestly, or a vintner, who adulterates the wine which he exposes for sale. Wycliffe renders it by an obsolete phrase, 'We are not of those who do avoutry the Word of God.' Tyndale renders it, 'We are not of those who chop and change the Word of God.' The Rhemish Version is, 'We are not as many, who adulterate the Word of God.' In our margin we read, 'We are not as many, who deal deceitfully with the Word of God.'

In the construction of the sentence, the Holy Ghost has inspired St Paul to use both the negative and the positive way of stating the truth. This mode of construction adds clearness and unmistakeableness to the meaning of the words, and intensity and strength to the assertion which they contain. Instances of a similar construction occur in three other remarkable passages of Scripture, two on the subject of baptism, one on the subject of the new birth. (*John* 1:13; *1 Pet.* 1:23, *1 Pet.* 3:21.) It will be found, therefore, that there are contained in the text both negative and positive lessons for the instruction of the ministers of Christ. Some things we ought to avoid. Others we ought to follow.

Negative Lessons

1. The first of the negative lessons is, *a plain warning against corrupting or dealing deceitfully with the Word of God.* The Apostle says, 'many' do it, pointing out to us that even in his time there were those who did not deal faithfully and honestly with God's truth. Here is a full answer to those who assert that the primitive Church was one of unmixed purity. The mystery of iniquity had already begun to work. The lesson which we are taught is, to beware of all dishonest statements of that Word of God which we are commissioned to preach. We are to add nothing to it. We are to take nothing away.

Now when can it be said of us that we corrupt the Word of God in the present day? What are the rocks and shoals which we ought to shun, if we would not be of the 'many' who deal deceitfully with God's truth? A few suggestions on this head may not be without use.

We corrupt the Word of God most dangerously, when we *throw any doubt on the plenary inspiration of any part of*

Holy Scripture. This is not merely corrupting the cup, but the whole fountain. This is not merely corrupting the bucket of living water, which we profess to present to our people, but poisoning the whole well.

Once wrong on this point, the whole substance of our religion is in danger. It is a flaw in the foundation. It is a worm at the root of our theology. Once allow this worm to gnaw the root, and we must not be surprised if the branches, the leaves, and the fruit, little by little decay.

The whole subject of inspiration, I am well aware, is surrounded with difficulty. All I would say is, that, in my humble judgment, notwithstanding some difficulties which we may not be able now to solve, the only safe and tenable ground to maintain is this, that every chapter, and every verse, and every word in the Bible has been 'given by inspiration of God'. We should never desert a great principle in theology any more than in science, because of apparent difficulties which we are not able at present to remove.

Suffer me to mention an illustration of this important axiom. Those conversant with astronomy know that, before the discovery of the planet Neptune there were difficulties, which greatly troubled the most scientific astronomers, respecting certain aberrations of the planet Uranus. These aberrations puzzled the minds of astronomers, and some of them suggested that they might possibly prove the whole Newtonian system to be untrue. But at that time a well-known French astronomer, named Leverrier, read before the Academy of Science a paper in which he laid down this great axiom, that it did not become a scientific man to give up a principle because of difficulties which could not be explained. He said in effect, 'We cannot explain the aberrations of Uranus now; but we may be sure that the Newtonian system will be proved to be right, sooner or later. Something may be discovered one day, which will prove that these aberrations may be accounted for, and yet the Newtonian system remain true and unshaken.'

A few years after, the anxious eyes of astronomers discovered the last great planet, Neptune. The planet was shown to be the true cause of all the aberrations of Uranus; and what the French astronomer had laid down as a principle in science, was proved to be wise and true. The application of the anecdote is obvious. Let us beware of giving up any first principle in theology. Let us not give up the great principle of plenary inspiration because of difficulties. The day may come when they will all be solved. In the mean time we may rest assured that the difficulties which beset any other theory of inspiration are tenfold greater than any which beset our own.

2. Secondly, we corrupt the Word of God when we *make defective statements of doctrine*. We do so when we add to

the Bible the opinions of the Church, or of the Fathers, as if they were of equal authority. We do so when we take away from the Bible, for the sake of pleasing men; or, from a feeling of false liberality, keep back any statement which seems narrow, and harsh, or hard. We do so when we try to soften down anything that is taught about eternal punishment, or the reality of hell. We do so when we bring forward doctrines in their wrong proportions.

We have all our favourite doctrines, and our minds are so constituted that it is hard to see one truth very clearly without forgetting that there are other truths equally important. We must not forget the exhortation of Paul, to minister 'according to the proportion of faith'.

We do so when we exhibit an excessive anxiety to fence, and guard, and qualify such doctrines as justification by faith without the deeds of the law, for fear of the charge of antinomianism; or when we flinch from strong statements about holiness, for fear of being thought legal.

We do so, not least, when we shrink from the use of Bible language in giving an account of doctrines. We are apt to keep back such expressions as 'born again', 'election', 'adoption', 'conversion', 'assurance', and to use a roundabout phraseology, as if we were ashamed of plain Bible words.

I cannot expand these statements, for want of time. I content myself with mentioning them, and leave them to your private thought.

3. In the third place, we corrupt the Word of God when we make *a defective practical application of it*. We do so when we do not discriminate between classes in our congregations – when we address all as being possessed of grace, by reason of their baptism or church-membership, and do not draw the line between those who have the Spirit and those who have not. Are we not apt to keep back plain home appeals to the unconverted? When we have eighteen hundred or two thousand persons before our pulpits, a vast proportion of whom we must know are unconverted, are we not apt to say, 'Now if there be any one of you who does not know the things that are for his eternal peace' – when we ought rather to say, 'If there be any of you who has not the grace of God in him'? And are we not in danger of defective handling of the Word in our practical exhortations by not bringing home the statements of the Bible to the various classes in our congregations? We speak plainly to the poor; but do we also speak plainly to the rich? Do we speak plainly in our dealings with the upper classes? This is a point on which, I fear, we need to search our consciences.

Positive Lessons

I now turn to the positive lessons which the text contains. '*As of sincerity, as of God, in the sight of God, speak we in Christ.*' A few words on each head must suffice.

We should aim to speak '*as of sincerity*' – sincerity of aim, heart, and motive, to speak as those who are thoroughly convinced of the truth of what they say; as those who have a deep feeling and tender love for those whom we address.

We should aim to speak '*as of God*'. We ought to strive to feel like men commissioned to speak for God, and on His behalf. In our dread of running into Romanism, we too often forget the language of the Apostle – 'I magnify mine office.' We forget how great is the responsibility of the New Testament minister, and how awful the sin of those who when a real messenger of Christ addresses them refuse to receive his message, and harden their hearts against it.

We should aim to speak as '*in the sight of God*'. We are to ask ourselves, not, What did the people think of me? but, What was I in the sight of God? Latimer was once called upon to preach before Henry VIII, and began his sermon in the following manner. (I quote from memory, and do not pretend to verbal accuracy.) He began: 'Latimer! Latimer! Dost thou remember thou art speaking before the high and mighty King Henry VIII; before him who has power to command thee to be sent to prison; before him who can have thy head struck off, if it please him? Wilt thou not take care to say nothing that will offend royal ears?' Then after a pause, he went on: 'Latimer! Latimer!

Dost not thou remember that thou art speaking before the King of kings and Lord of lords; before Him, at whose bar Henry VIII will stand; before Him to whom one day thou wilt have to give account thyself? Latimer! Latimer! Be faithful to thy Master, and declare all God's Word.' Oh, that this may be the spirit in which we may ever retire from our pulpits, not caring whether men are pleased or displeased, not caring whether men say we were eloquent or feeble; but going away with the witness of our conscience, 'I have spoken as in God's sight.'

Finally, we should aim to speak '*as in Christ*'. The meaning of this phrase is doubtful. Grotius says, 'We are to speak as in His name, as ambassadors.' But Grotius is poor authority. Beza says, 'We are to speak about Christ, concerning Christ.' This is good doctrine, but hardly the meaning of the words. Others say, We are to speak as ourselves joined to Christ, as those who have received mercy from Christ, and whose only title to address others is from Christ alone. Others say, We should speak as through Christ, in the strength of Christ. No meaning, perhaps, is better than this. The expression in the Greek exactly answers to Philippians 4:13, 'I can do all things through Christ, which strengtheneth me.'

Whatever sense we ascribe to these words, one thing is clear: we should speak in Christ, as those who have themselves received mercy; as those who desire to exalt, not themselves, but the Saviour; and as those who care nothing what men think of them, so long as Christ is magnified in their ministry.

In conclusion, we should all inquire, Do we ever handle the Word of God deceitfully? Do we realize what it is to speak as of God, as in the sight of God, and in Christ?

Let me put to all one searching question. Is there any text in God's Word which we shrink from expounding? Is there any statement in the Bible which we avoid speaking about to our people, not because we do not understand it, but because it contradicts some pet notion of ours as to what is truth? If it be so, let us ask our consciences whether this be not very like handling the Word of God deceitfully.

Is there anything in the Bible we keep back for fear of seeming harsh, and of giving offence to some of our hearers? Is there any statement, either doctrinal or practical, which we mangle, mutilate or dismember? If so, are we dealing honestly with God's Word?

Let us pray to be kept from corrupting God's Word. Let neither fear nor favour of man induce us to keep back, or avoid, or change, or mutilate, or qualify any text in the Bible. Surely we ought to have holy boldness when we speak as ambassadors of God. We have no reason to be ashamed of any statement we make in our pulpits so long as it is Scriptural. I have often thought that one great secret of the marvellous honour which God has put on a man who is not in our communion (I allude to Mr Spurgeon), is the extraordinary boldness and confidence with which he stands up in the pulpit to speak to people about their sins and their souls. It cannot be said he does it from fear of any, or to please any. He seems to give every class of hearers its portion, to the rich and the poor, the high and the low, the peer and the peasant, the learned and the illiterate. He gives to every one plain dealing, according to God's Word.

I believe that very boldness has much to do with the success which God is pleased to give to his ministry. Let us not be ashamed to learn a lesson from him in this respect. Let us go and do likewise.